Through It All We're Still Standing

Empowered and Triumphant Through Adversity

**Presented by
Judith Johnson-Hostler**

& co-authors Gina Davis, Debra McKinney Hill, Sylvia James, Robin Langhorne, Gladys "Cookie" Payton, Vallori Thomas, and Electra Fowler Willis

Copyright © 2021 by Judith Johnson-Hostler

All rights reserved. This book or any portion thereof may not be reproduced or used in any manner whatsoever without the express written permission of the publisher except for the use of brief quotations in a book review or scholarly journal.

ISBN: 978-1-7379629-1-5
First Printing: 2021

Ordering Information:
Special discounts are available on quantity purchases by corporations, associations, educators, and others. For details, contact the publisher at the above-listed address.

U.S. trade bookstores and wholesalers: Please contact info@businessofbooksmastermind.com

DEDICATION

This book is dedicated to the memory of our beloved sister, friend, and confidant Marcia Hayes-Miller. For being the example of recovery in the face of adversity and in times of uncertainty. Marcia embodied courage, valor, and strength. She will be remembered for the lives she touched, for her laughter and fabulous birthday parties. For all the cafeteria lunch sessions, trips to Atlantic City, church attendance, and her courageous journey with cancer. Her admiration for family and friends was unparalleled. She leaves a legacy for her three beautiful daughters, two grandsons and siblings. Also, for her other relatives, and friends to treat everyone better than you want to be treated and to live your life to the fullest.

Table of Contents

DEDICATION iv

ACKNOWLEDGMENTS vi

PREFACE 1

LIST OF AUTHORS IN CHAPTER ORDER 2

THE THIRD 3

YOU WILL NEVER BE LEFT IN THE DARK 10

DREAM CHASER 18

LOST AND FOUND 25

FROM IMPOSSIBLE TO I'M POSSIBLE 34

VISIBLY INVISIBLE 40

BLESSED BEYOND MEASURE 46

CHOICES 58

ABOUT THE LEAD AUTHOR 66

ACKNOWLEDGMENTS

I would first like to honor God for the great things that he has done for each of us. We are beyond overjoyed that we could share our journey with the world.

I want to acknowledge all the phenomenal women that were a part of this amazing process. It was a journey that we will never forget. The patience that you all exhibited during his process helped us move forward.

I believe and know that this project will catapult each one of you to even greater heights. I am excited to see what will come forth due to your obedience in birthing this project.

I would like to thank the publishing company Business of Books Mastermind for your guidance and support during this process. Being able to have our needs met at one company helped streamline the success of our venture. We enjoyed working with you.

PREFACE

This phenomenal book is based on lived experiences. Its pages may speak to some of the challenging experiences that you may have faced or, if not you, someone you know. The writers display through their stories that it takes great courage and tenacity to hold on until a storm has passed.

You will find in the center of the cover there is a picture of a palm tree with the sun in all its glory. In comparison to other trees, the palm tree appears fragile and weak, unable to weather the storms. However, just the opposite is true; palm trees represent **resilience.**

Similar to the writer's stories, the palm tree's roots burrow deep in a storm. From a biblical perspective, the palm tree has spiritual attributes and symbolic meaning. It symbolizes freedom, righteousness, reward, resurrection, victory, and returning happily from a journey.

The co-authors in this book have weathered storms that could have or should have killed them. From drug addictions, family curses, and childhood trauma. To cancer, divorce, loss of relationships, hopelessness, etc. With GOD's grace like the palm tree through it all, they still stand.

LIST OF AUTHORS IN CHAPTER ORDER

1. Gladys "Cookie" Payton
2. Judith Johnson-Hostler
3. Gina Davis
4. Sylvia James
5. Vallori Thomas
6. Electra Fowler-Willis
7. Debra McKinney-Hill
8. Robin Langhorne

THE THIRD

Gladys "Cookie" Payton

Gladys Gertrude Payton III. Go ahead, you can say it again. Gladys Gertrude Payton III. This is me, a third-generation Gladys! I am named after both my maternal and paternal grandmothers. I got one name from each. It's my birth name and I also believe that it has been my superpower—a kind of strength that has covered me. My name has carried me through my trauma, drama. It has guided me through my addiction, depression, and unbelievable life accomplishments. My name is my light that shines. I reflect on this because I am also called Cookie. It was my dad who gave me that name.

It was November 12, 2013—eleven, twelve, thirteen. On this day I was forever changed. I experienced a sort of resurrection that gave me a new outlook on my life and God. On November 12, 2013, my doorbell rang at 4 a.m. It was my niece. She had come to my house to go with us to the hospital for my scheduled surgery to remove both my breasts, a double mastectomy. That July I got diagnosed with breast cancer. At that first meeting with my doctor to go over the results, all I remember her saying was "carcinoma."

Everything else to me from that point was foggy, wonk, wonk, wonk, like the voices in Charlie Brown. Thank goodness my sister and niece were there with a pen and pad so they could go over everything with me later at home. Devastated, all I could think was, "You are going to die!"

I stayed in a funk for a while before I began to feel something else: "No. You can't die—you have to live!"

In the months following my diagnosis, I became somewhat of an expert on breast cancer. And I was on information overload. I was still struggling with accepting that I had cancer when I had to decide if having a mastectomy was the best option. Then it became a question of having both my breasts removed. There was so much information out there, but what would be the right thing for me? The thought of having my breasts removed was horrifying. As a woman, I thought of my breasts as my womanhood.

It was my best friend, who was in stage IV cancer at that time, who helped me. I remember many of our talks and cries when she would have her cancer surgeries and treatments. My best friend told me this: "If having your breast removed allows you to live and lessens the chances of cancer coming back, then DO IT! In fact, go ahead and do them both now so that you won't worry about having one removed and then having to go through it all over again, like me." I loved, trusted my best friend, and decided that I would go ahead and have both breasts removed. In my heart I know that was the best choice for me.

I awoke from surgery with my family standing over me. From the look on their faces, I knew something was wrong. Even my sister, the nurse had this perplexed look on her face. The plan was to remove both breasts. Then another surgeon would come in and do the reconstruction. Seeing their faces, I asked what happened and was thinking – well am I dead? No one said anything. I turned to my niece who at that time was in medical school. She was with me every step of the way.

I said, "Tell me what happened!"

She told me that my surgery lasted much longer than expected. I was also under anesthesia longer than the doctors were comfortable with. My surgery lasted for fourteen hours. Everybody was in shock that I woke up and was able to speak! There was a sigh of relief and laughter. I remember somebody saying, "Oh, okay, she's good—back to her normal bossy self." I'm sure it was my oldest sister and my mom.

That night or at least sometime after my family left, I woke up again. This time I could hardly breathe and could feel a heaviness around me. I thought I was gonna die. God showed up. Until this day I don't know if it was a nurse or an angel sent from heaven. But this woman appeared and she sat me up to open my airway so I could breathe. She bathed me and I remember her hands being so gentle and soothing. I couldn't speak, but I was so grateful for her care. It felt like God's grace, and I was so grateful for the love and to be alive. I call that moment the beginning of my life shift.

I started to heal in the physical but a few months after my surgery, one thing after the other began to happen. It was a series of unfortunate events that would happen for me, and not to me. For me because most people believe that when pain occurs something bad is happening to them. What I have found is some things happen to cause us pain but they can also sharpen and develop us in ways never imagined. This explains what I think of as God's will.

The first unfortunate event was that my partner had become very detached from me. I spoke with my therapist about it and she said this happens many times in relationships. Partners of cancer patients also experience an effect from it. They can become very uncomfortable with touching and handling you. As if you were fragile and might break. The other thing she had seen is some partners try and escape their feelings through working a lot, some even turn to someone else for comfort.

The love and support that I got from my family, and my friends were incredible. They showered me with so much love and support but I felt guilty like as if I had a choice in it and they didn't deserve cancer. My mom, who was in her late seventies, was there when I got home from the hospital. She nursed me back to health. I am blessed and loved. Unfortunately, my partner continued to detach. Since he refused to communicate what he was going through, I had to make a decision. I chose myself. It was more important to heal myself than to fall into a cycle of trying to figure out what I could do to make him feel better about my cancer. I came to find out that he had been having an affair. He would come home after being out all night, and proclaim his unhappiness.

"I am not happy, and I haven't been for a long time," he said.

I had been struggling with what was going on with him, so at this point, I was ready to accept it. I could no longer fight to live and fight his inability to cope.

I surrendered and told him, "Then do what you need to be happy." He left that day.

This would leave me alone in my home with only my dog Madiba. A house that a year ago my godchildren lived on one floor, my best friend on the second, and me and my family on the third floor. This is a house that we had rehabbed and turned into a home. Those years surrounded by my friends and family in that home were some of the best of my life. Now everyone has moved out and moved on including my children. I was empty nesting and also left alone in an empty house. It took several weeks before I could even muster the will to move on. I suffered physically, emotionally, financially, and spiritually.

Depression ran deep. By this time, I'd survived the breast removal surgery and my family returned to living their lives. As a woman, the emotional toll of having my breasts removed was horrific. Then to have my partner move on to another woman as if he had no regard for our relationship and no remorse—added insult to injury. I felt betrayed. I couldn't stay in that house anymore. I had to leave.

Just two months after moving, I was on to the next unfortunate event. I returned to my job to find out that my position no longer existed. This was a job that I served for over twenty years. I loved working for a national organization whose mission was to empower the underserved. My mother's sister was at the helm and she had grown this company into a multi-million-dollar business. We often disagreed about a lot of things, but my Aunty had been my Shero! She was my friend, my boss, my sister, my mentor, and my confidant. She became my go-to during and after my struggles with addiction. I always wanted to make her proud and I believe I did.

Seeking strength and guidance I joined a support group at my church. We would meet every Sunday after church service with our pastor. Our group had become so close. It was a "no judgment" zone and we were able to be open and honest about anything we were going through. My pastor was somewhat of a comedian so even though we shed a lot of tears, much of our healing was through laughter. I mean fall out, cracking up, stomach hurting, genuine laughter. It was such a unique group. We would always somehow be able to turn our trauma into laughter.

My pastor was highly educated, well respected and one of the humblest people I'd ever met. He was unapologetic about his truth and had an anointing that made you feel comfortable in your own skin. One morning I got a call that my pastor died in his chambers. The very office we would take our shoes off if we wanted, eat, and have our meetings. My pastor was the truth! He poured so much love into us. He had such a presence about him that whenever we were around him, I'd always feel like his favorite - we all did.

I began to struggle with my losses. My breasts, my relationship, my home, my Aunty, my job, and my pastor. I felt like I had lost my life and my mind. At this point, I knew that everything in my life has changed forever. For a while I was stuck. I was afraid to live. Afraid that I would lose. That I just could not survive any more hits. Remembering a discussion, I once had with my dad led me to find gratitude yet again.

He said, "Cookie, it's great that you have good childhood memories, but now you have to create some new ones." Since I didn't want to die my only other option was to live. I will live my life to the fullest creating new memories.

"To thine own self be true," another gem Daddy dropped on me. But it was so hard. You see, I can take care, show up, and get motivated for you. But for the first time, all I needed was to be responsible for myself. It's one of the most difficult things I've ever had to do, but through it all, I'm still standing and to thine own self I shall be true. I choose happiness. I choose life. I choose me. (The beginning).

ABOUT THE AUTHOR:
Social Media:
IG instagram.com/thatmycookie/
FB facebook.com/cookie.payton.9
Website Address xxx
Email Cpay007@gmail.com

Gladys "Cookie" Payton is a graduate of St. Peters University. Gladys holds a Bachelor's Degree in Urban Studies with an emphasis on Public Policy. By trade, Gladys is a Licensed Practical Nurse, Realtor, General Contractor, and Serial Entrepreneur. She is the founder of GG3 Development LLC, a Real Estate Development, Project Management, and Consulting firm; and Lashed Queens Wigs LLC, a Medical Wig Supplier, Human Hair Vendor, and Custom Wig Making company. Gladys holds numerous awards and certifications.

Gladys' professional experience includes small business development, education, training, health, and beauty. She is an expert in helping communities, families, and individuals transition from crisis to self-sufficiency, building new and healthy futures. Gladys has also developed and implemented programs in the areas of homeownership, financial literacy, construction training, mentorship, small business development, job placement, childcare, family counseling, and programs for seniors.

Gladys is also a breast cancer survivor. Her journey with breast cancer experience in navigating our healthcare system and the effects of an illness, financial and otherwise, has deepened her passion for helping build strong and healthy families, individuals, and communities.

Gladys Payton 'Cookie,' is a divorced mother of two children SuQuan and Brittany. She has one granddaughter, Emory Briar, and god-daughter A'kela.

YOU WILL NEVER BE LEFT IN THE DARK

Judith Johnson-Hostler

In the dead of Winter December 8, 2009, I drove to work traveling South on the New Jersey Turnpike/Garden State Parkway. There was an eerie silence in my car as I headed to work. The phone rang through the car; I answered, and I couldn't believe what I was being told on the other end. It was Bank of America informing me that for over ninety days my mortgage was past due. I asked all the necessary questions to confirm that this was the absolute truth. Did my husband, who always handled the bills without fail, not pay the mortgage? I hung up with the bank with the intent to call him immediately; I was totally confused and needed to know what was going on.

Immediately when I hung up, the phone rang again, and this time it was my daughter ranting and raging about last night. I made it clear to her that I will not take her disrespect. If she plans to continue to live at home, the behavior that she has been displaying lately needs to completely change. My daughter has a very young baby at home, only five months old. It had been challenging to express to her that once you have a child that your life as you knew it completely changes.

It seemed that my phone was ringing off the hook, the phone rang again. This time the call was from my husband. He began to talk about some nonsense that made no sense to me.

He said, "I thought that we could get a divorce split the annuity, and then remarry."

I was utterly at a loss because why did we need our pension right now? I was not aware that we were having any financial problems. He was talking so fast that I didn't even have an opportunity to ask him about our mortgage. Dazed by his conversation I hung up before mentioning the call from Bank of America.

Immediately when we hung- up, I began to have an overload of thoughts, and my mind started to playback different thoughts and scenes in my mind. It all started coming together. I began to recognize that there had been some changes in his schedule, his behavior, and change in his cell phone usage. Very clearly, I heard a voice say he is cheating on you; what are you going to do. The bank is already using threatening language. They want their money, your daughter is acting out, with all this going on, you will be highly humiliated in your little big city, Asbury Park. The people in your town look up to you two as a power couple; shame will follow whatever his little secret is.

The next voice was an audible voice that said, you can't live through all of this; you should just crash into that divider on the Parkway. Slow down because when you hit the wall, you need to time it perfectly so your car retracts from the partition and hits the truck to the right. The impact of such a crash will kill you immediately. My next thought was, devil, you are a liar; you will not take my life; my God has plans for me.

My next call was to my girlfriend (sister). I was crying hysterically, trying to tell her through all of the wailing and screaming what was going on. I managed to slow down my fast rapid speech. I told her my husband was cheating on me. I told her about the call from Bank of America and the bizarre conversation that I had with my husband. I told her about the very vivid audible voice that was telling me to take my life.

My friend told me to pull over to get my composure. She reminded me to breathe. Then we began to pray and ask God to come in and help me through this impossible situation. A calm came over me; I remember that God has me, and no matter what the problem is, I'm going to get through it. The Bible reminds us, Philippians 4:13, "I can do all things through Christ who strengthens me" (KJV).

Once I made it through all the confusion spinning through my head, I made it to my office. I walked in the door of my place of employment. I didn't open my mouth to anyone at work about what was going. However, my job was a place that I felt safe if I needed to share these issues. My head was spinning; what's next. I just sat at my desk praying, taking deep breaths, and allowing God's spirit to bring peace in what felt like chaos.

A day in August a few months before this day I was hanging in my room doing homework. The assignment was for my counseling course in my graduate program at Monmouth University of Long Branch, New Jersey. Now at the time, I was in my right mind; I heard a very quiet voice say get up, I want to take you somewhere. The voice led me turn by turn to Brighton Arm Apartments. I had a cousin that lived there and my brother-in-law, but I wasn't there to see either of them. The next thought was very clear, now look for your husband's truck to the right of you, your friend's daughter lives here. I left Brighton Arms none the wiser because I didn't entertain the thought of my husband ever cheating on me; I never thought about that day again.

As my morning progressed, I connected that unexplainable event in August to this very chilly day in December. The next thing to do was find a way to access his phone to hear his voicemail and obtain his text messages. I have never done anything like this because I couldn't imagine this would ever happen to us. I got access to all his messages. I sat at my desk holding back my tears. It was my friend's daughter. This twenty-one-year-old girl and the filth that was on the voicemail and text messages blew my mind. I felt and thought to myself, how could he? This man is double her age.

What are my next steps? I printed the text messages and highlighted the days and the times. Most of these calls were all day when he was at work and I was at school, or Sundays when we were at church. He not only disrespected me, but he called his girlfriend as he sat next to the pastor. I guess it didn't faze him that he was a leader in the church. I walked in the door with my mind racing and raging, ready to hear what this dude had to say to explain such a thing. When I approached him, he had a half-smirk on his face, with a look of relief that it was finally out. I asked him to explain how something like this has happened to us. Of course, he tried to lie and tell me that it wasn't the truth. All I could think of in the days and the months that followed was that half-smirk on his face. I was so hurt by his disregard for my feelings. The enemy has crept into my home without my acknowledgment. The one thing I can trust is that God had and still has my back.

That very evening my son was anxiously waiting for me.

He said, "Mom, can we talk? I have to tell you something that's going to hurt you. My dad is cheating on you with your friend's daughter. He had the speakerphone on, and I could hear her voice when I put my ear to the door."

My son said it took him some time to get his nerve up to tell me. He sat there and wept, his little heartbroken because his dad was his superhero. When infidelity occurs, it is an offense to the entire family. It's a web that spreads wide. It crushed my children. My nieces and nephews, our home was their second home, and it devastated them as well. The kids in the neighborhood, our church family, our community, and our friends all saw it as a personal attack on me and on them. When unfaithfulness creeps in, the individual or individuals usually don't play the entire tape; they just roll with what's in front of them, "LUST."

The enemy has a personal attack on families. Today we see fewer and fewer marriages work. Especially in the African American community. The rates of divorce are even higher in Christian families. We often hear the chatter, why would I waste my time and money on marriage? It doesn't work. Marriage does work, but like anything else, you must work at it.

For me, I was in total shock because I was constantly pouring into my relationship and myself. We often did things like date night, couples' events, and marriage retreats. The key is, it takes two. Don't get me wrong, I am not saying if one spouse is not engaging physically, emotionally, and mentally the other should stop. No, not at all, you keep fighting for your marriage! In my case, I felt as if I was sucker-punched, or shall I use an old-school word—bamboozled. But as I mentioned, I was not left in the dark. I was being prepared; I just didn't know it.

I was a member at a phenomenal church—Macedonia. The presiding pastor, Tommy D. Miles, and my spirit was being fed during this season. My connection to a powerful women's ministry at Triumphant Life in Asbury Park— also fostered my growth in the word. On the first Friday of every month, they held a meet and greet fellowship called the Leading Ladies. We spent time getting to know one another and delving deep into God's word. I remember their last women's conference before December 2009.

Their visiting preacher looked at me and said, "You are leaving this place. I am not talking about this church; I'm talking about your life as you know it."

My marriage didn't work, and I absolutely didn't listen to the devil encouraging me to take my life. The visiting preacher prophesied that I was leaving everything I know, and I did just that. As she said, my life as I knew it was changing. On August 28, 2010, I moved to Raleigh, North Carolina, to the sweet smell of the South. A couple of days before the move, a few of my girlfriends came over. I was in my empty house lying on the floor crying and looking pitiful.

They said, "Girl, get up from there, people need you to get up and live."

I got up and wiped my tears, and said out loud, "God please help move me forward."

In 2014 I married the love of my life, Robert Hostler. We have been friends for many years and are from the same hometown Asbury Park, New Jersey. As I prepared for my wedding, I went to my beautician to touch up my hair, and guess what it started to rain. Every woman's nightmare is rain on her wedding day. With her beautiful spirit, my beautician reminded me that God is in charge.

She said, "The rain is His way of reminding me that He is washing away the old, the pain, the hurt, and the distrust." From those sweet words from my beautician (my friend), I changed my perspective of the rain on that day, and then the sun came out in its full glory. Our family and friends traveled from near and far to share on our beautiful day as we became one. Enemy, you lose again, marriage is important and it requires work.

I must share all the blessings that God has given me because I held on. I have a happy and healthy marriage, eleven grand loves, my children are working through all that occurred. Still, like everything else, God has shown me He will get the glory. I trust God will restore and heal my children from the hurt and all that occurred. My husband is an ordained Elder, and I am a licensed Evangelist. We are the directors of member's services at our church and leaders in the marriage ministry. I have obtained two master's degrees in counseling. I am a licensed clinical mental health counselor (LCMHC), a licensed clinical addiction specialist (LCAS). I also am a national certified counselor (NCC). All credentials mentioned occurred after 2009, and I won't forget a host of friends and family that supported me through it all. I can't forget one of the biggest things God did for me, on June 13, 2021, I celebrated thirty years of recovery!

In closing, I must remind you and myself that I hold on for dear life as I go through tough times and that God never leaves me in the dark. My relationship with God and life took on a different meaning. In mentioning all these blessings and accolades I am not bragging on myself but bragging on God. We go through but God has shown me if I hold on, He will give me the victory, that's right, THROUGH IT ALL, I AM STILL STANDING!!!

ABOUT THE AUTHOR:

Social Media:
IG instagram.com/judejj65/
FB facebook.com/jude.johnsonhostler
Website Address https://denomealliances.com/
Email journeytohigherheights@gmail.com

Services offered:

Therapy, coaching, public speaking, conference planning, and retreat planning.

For Judith's full bio, please see the about the author section at the end.

DREAM CHASER

Gina Davis

As a clinical social worker, licensed and certified in different areas, I have the pleasure of helping people find their voice. I help them speak their truths and engage in the healing process. The story I'm sharing with you today is part of my life experience, speaking my truth. My hope is to encourage you to continue or get started on chasing your dreams. I believe you or someone you know will be able to move from survivor to thriver after reading this book.

I grew up as a middle child in a family of nine. It wasn't the perfect family (alcohol problems and living below the poverty level), but we loved each other and I have a lot of great memories. It was clear to everyone that mom was in charge of overseeing the household. Her philosophy was if her children were going to get into trouble, they were gonna get into trouble at home. Like every proud mama, she had good intentions and wanted nothing but the best for her children.

I made her proud by receiving straight A's in grammar school. I continued having excellent grades in intermediate school (middle school) with little effort. So, she trusted me to complete chores, run errands, and handle other delicate matters as needed. She took pride in my abilities and often bragged about my many accomplishments and trustworthiness. She could often be overheard saying, "But not my Gina—not her!" in a bragging tone. She didn't recognize the low self-esteem, low self-worth or my introverted personality, and negative feelings of being less than that I held on the inside.

Despite how I felt inside, I still knew I wanted to be somebody when I grew up. I dreamed of graduating from high school and going to college; something no one in my family of origin had ever accomplished. I was the dream chaser!

Entering high school, I struggled because I felt emotionally and socially inept. I felt unprepared for the new challenges since my older siblings had already dropped out. Somehow, I did manage to survive my freshman year. However, as a sophomore, my social anxiety increased and I struggled with attending class. I found myself hanging out in the second-floor girls' bathroom. On most days smoking cigarettes and/or weed and getting suspended for cutting class.

On my final trip to the vice principal's office with my mother at my side, Mr. Hartman stated he was "tired of seeing me" and no longer wanted to see me in his office.

My mother, looking me straight in the eyes, said, "And I am tired of bringing you back to school."

Without any hesitation or thought, I responded, "And I'm tired of walking to school. So, I will do you both a favor, I'll quit." It still baffles me to this day why neither of the adults in the room made any attempt to encourage me to continue with my education.

As I was being escorted by the school's security officer to remove my personal property from the locker, I had an overwhelming sense of loss. I wanted to take that irrational decision back but pride wouldn't allow me to humble myself. I voluntarily withdrew from high school at sixteen years old.

Lesson learned: Just because you can doesn't mean you should! Pride will help you to soar to heights beyond your imagination. However, false pride will kill your dreams right in its tracks!

The unspoken message I received from that one act was that nobody cared and I was old enough to make my own decisions. Things changed quickly, within a matter of months. During my first sexual encounter, I became pregnant and at seventeen years old I delivered my first child. Uneducated, unskilled, unemployable, and now a single parent on welfare. I would deliver another child two years later. Over the next seven years, I would become the mother of four children. I loved my children but I was very disappointed in myself, for bringing them into the world without the means to provide for them. Over the years I made the choice to sell drugs to support my family. Consequently, I got caught and went to jail.

Lesson learned: There is no right way to do the wrong thing!

Selling drugs worked for a while but the time came when I didn't recognize myself. I looked in the mirror and I didn't see the girl who wanted to be somebody when she grew up. I had lost any trace of her and I was no longer the dealer, I had become the user!

I didn't like the person I had become and I wanted to die! Though I wasn't suicidal. I internalized self-hatred and thought everyone else and things would be better off if I were dead. Drugs had robbed me of my dignity, pride, self-respect, and the ability to provide self-care or care of my four children.

Lesson learned: Drugs have the power to change you into someone I was never intended to be!

Divine intervention comes in many forms including pain. One day in my absence my youngest child, three years old, experienced a seizure and was taken to the emergency room by ambulance, with a family friend and was admitted to the hospital.

The hospital contacted child protection services and was informed to alert them when the mom showed up. Three days after the hospital admission I showed up and the worker was contacted. She took one look at me and said she could not release her to me and my daughter entered the foster-care system. This was the event that changed the direction of my life, as there was nothing more important in this world to me than my children and family. The pain of losing my child was unbearable.

Lesson Learned: The crushing comes before the oil!

I made the decision to get help and on December 17, 1989, I entered a residential rehabilitation program. While in rehab the twelve steps would introduce me to the concept of a higher power, GOD. Initially, I was afraid to pray or call on God because my beliefs in God came from dogma. God doesn't like ugly and I sure was ugly, and God will strike you down, etc. I recognize still today people will weaponize God to their advantage not considering the harm they may be causing.

I found a loving and caring GOD in rehab who had been with me the entire time. Yes, in the principal's office, in a jail cell, in the hospital, and even in the throes of my addiction.

Lesson learned: GOD is with me!

Going to rehab interrupted my cycle of addiction, but the twelve-step fellowship of Narcotics Anonymous changed my life! I gained a better understanding of who I was, why, and how I lost my way. The fellowship didn't give me back my old life, it offered me hope and a new way to live. It ignited the fire inside of me and I am happy to say, today I am a dream chaser!

My daughter was returned to my custody immediately after completing the twenty-eight-day rehabilitation program.

I returned to school and I am the first in my family of origin to earn a college degree.

I met the love of my life in 1989, we dated five years and then married in 1995.

Lesson Learned: "Old dreams are reawakened and new possibilities arise" (Narcotics Anonymous).

In my process of recovery, there have been many disappointments, upsets, and adversities: a medical crisis in 2017, I had brain surgery to remove a cerebral aneurysm; 2016 the death of my husband (cancer). Over the course of a decade, I experienced the deaths of my parents, grandparents, five siblings, three nephews, a niece, other relatives, and numerous friends. Some of these losses were anticipated, others suddenly and then there were those that were tragic and out of timing.

It saddens me to think that neither of my deceased siblings ever reached my current age and to know that I will grow old without them. Life on life's terms.

Whether by default or destiny I have emerged as the matriarch in my family of origin, and I proudly accept the mantle. I will speak of them and tell their stories to the next generation(s), for I am grateful to be alive. Through it all, I still stand!

Lesson Learned: GOD has a plan for my life.

If you are an adolescent, a mom, caregiver, an adult with influence or authority to shape someone else's life and you are on the sidelines or on the fence, doubting yourself or giving up, (on yourself or someone else). Don't give up before miracles begin to happen. There is nothing you cannot do when you commit to doing it. Just think about it, what have you committed yourself (100%) to doing that you weren't able to accomplish? Breathe life into the situation and get to chasing your dreams!

Lesson Learned: "Any addict can stop using drugs, lose the desire to use, and find a new way of life" (Narcotics Anonymous).

ABOUT THE AUTHOR:
Social Media:
FB facebook.com/gina.davis.3975
Website Address www.resetplace.com
Email ginadavis-lane@resetplace.com

A native of Asbury Park, New Jersey, Gina has more than twenty-five years of professional experience working in the fields of Social Work and Addiction Counseling. She is an entrepreneur, independent practitioner, and the sole proprietor of Reset Place Assessment and Counseling Center in Neptune NJ. She is a therapist and educator Specializing in Substance Use Disorders, Grief, Trauma, and Recovery.

Davis received her Associate's Degree in Human Services at Brookdale Community College, Lincroft, NJ; Bachelor's Degree in Social Work at Kean University, Union, NJ and Master's Degree in Social Work at Fordham University, New York (Lincoln Center).

Gina has also attended the RAPT Training Program and received her Certification and Licensure as Alcohol and Drug Counselor (CADC/LCADC). Davis completed the Grief Recovery Method Training and received her Certification as a Grief Recovery Specialist and Educator. She also brings her professional expertise to the work environment.

In her personal time, she enjoys visiting with her four children, eleven grandchildren, and extended family members.

LOST AND FOUND

Sylvia James

I was born in Camden, New Jersey where I lived for the first thirty years of my life. As a child growing up, I found myself spending a lot of time alone. I didn't have any friends, but I would hang out with my cousins sometimes. Other kids teased me as a child because we were poor. My mother was on welfare, she was barely able to take care of me and my two younger siblings. I would see neighborhood children with two-parent households and often wondered what that was like. I didn't stay there too long in my imagination, I just moved on knowing that was only a fantasy for me. I found myself using fantasy a lot as a way of escape from what was going on around me.

I loved to write as a child, and reading books was another way I escaped into a fantasy all my own. I could be whomever I chose to be within my own mind and my own world. That took away some of the pain I felt about things that were happening around me. I often wondered where my father was, and why he was not there for me. When asking the question, I never got a clear answer. One day I stopped asking so many questions because I was told to stay in a child's place. It was during that time I learned that asking questions got me into trouble. I did not want to get chastised for being "grown," and not following directions. Getting beatings was the form of discipline used in my household, and I did not want to get hit. I knew talking back was disrespectful. I was not able to voice my views or opinions. I simply went along with anything told to me. I was never asked how or what I felt. So, I learned at an early age how to suppress my feelings.

The hardest part for me was not knowing how to use my voice, especially when it came to other people. That was a learned behavior that went along with the thoughts of the elders, that children were to be seen and not heard. That thought process scarred me, as I grew up, I felt unheard and unseen. I didn't think anything I had to say was important. I was also taught, what happened in my household stayed in the house. That taught me how to keep secrets, my own, and others. When terrible things were happening to me and around me, I could not tell anyone about it. I kept all that stuff inside and it festered within me as a child. I began to act out a lot as I got older, it was my way of expressing what I had felt for so long.

As a teenager, I got myself into trouble as most teenagers do. I was sneaking out of the house, and hanging out with people my mother did not agree with. Before middle school I did not have any friends, so I just wanted to fit in with my schoolmates and have fun as I saw them doing. To me, I was just being a teenager, I didn't feel I was doing anything wrong. My mother felt differently and was not having it. She asked me to leave her house, she put me out. I was fourteen years old. Although I was not listening and wanted to do my own thing, I did go to school and was a good student, I always got good grades. I guess that wasn't enough. For years I harbored resentments about that situation.

The anger I felt was so intense, words could not describe it. I could not understand what was happening in my life, what was wrong with me. What had I done that was so bad? I had so many unanswered questions. I became angry with God, I always felt he heard the prayers of others, but never mine. The bitterness I felt ran deep, disgusted with myself, I just could not make sense of it all. I can remember saying, I just want this pain to stop. It was unbearable the weight I carried. How did I get here? I would ask myself repeatedly until it just didn't matter anymore "how". I told myself I had to change my mindset, I had to figure things out. I had very little preparation for what was to come.

My life was spiraling out of control. All I could tell myself is that I needed to be strong. I held on for as long as I could before I began to slip away from myself into someone I didn't even know anymore. I was so hurt, I felt betrayed, disowned, and devalued. I had no one I could turn to, everyone was living their own lives and dealing with their problems. This is where I learned that I could not depend on anyone but myself. I had gotten to a place where the only emotion I could get in touch with was anger, and it was very intense, I had no clue what to do. I had no idea what was to come, I did know it was going to get harder for me before it got better.

I was so frustrated and heartbroken, I remember sitting outside on a step, holding my head, crying, and praying to God asking Him what was happening to me. I cried and cried hoping someone would come to rescue me from the pain and myself. Unfortunately, no one ever came. Everywhere I turned seeking help, direction, or guidance; those people had ulterior motives. That was the place where I learned a little more about relationships. I learned that the old cliché of give and take was not true. In fact, my relationships were quite one-sided, and in my experience—painful. Being at a place where I needed people, and they knew this, they took advantage where they could. Those were the situations that began to shape my attitude negatively toward people and life itself.

This is where I learned life was hard, cruel, and conditional. It was during that time I learned how to work my way around my circumstances. I did the best I could, however, I made some big mistakes. I surrounded myself with older people, looking for a role model. I needed a savior, someone who would help me navigate my way during one of the toughest times of my life. And yet again, what I found were people who used me and took advantage of me. I was so lost, however, I had faith that my life would not always be that way. There was something inside of me that kept me going, and directed me when I had come to what I thought was the end of the road.

Over the years many things took place, I began having children, and being a mother was one of the best things that happened for me. In my mind, I had children who were going to love me unconditionally. Needless to say, I screwed that up too. I put my children through a lot. Things continued to get worse, I said I wanted the pain to stop, however, I kept creating circumstances for myself. At twenty-four years old, I started doing drugs. I snorted cocaine, smoked laced cigarettes, and eventually, those behaviors led to my smoking crack cocaine. It was all downhill from there, I thought my life was a mess before this, once I started getting high, I really found out what bad was. I sank fast like I was standing in quicksand going down quickly. There was no coming back, I had found what I needed to make the pain go away. So, I thought.

The greatest fall came in my life when I lost my children. I had many people who stated they wanted to support me; however, their support was not supportive to me. It was very judgmental, degrading, and situational. This is the place where negative things were said to me, and about me. I had a sour taste in my mouth for people altogether. Being at such a low place in my life I learned I had many relatives and not much family. There was no compassion, but hey, how can people have concern for something they don't understand or had never encountered.

With everything I had experienced, I eventually had enough. I no longer wanted to live the way that I was. Honestly, I had lost everything that meant anything to me, the only thing I had to lose at that point was my life. To hear me tell it, I wasn't that lucky, I needed to suffer for whatever reasons. I was sick and tired of being sick and tired of me. I was ready to change, I committed to wanting better for myself. I didn't know how it was going to happen, but what I did know was that it was not going to happen for me in the city of Camden. I knew I needed to leave, I needed to go away to give myself a chance at a better life. I knew who I had become was not who I was. People only saw the outside, I had a clever idea of who was on the inside of me, I just needed to find her. For the first time in my life, I had goals, dreams, and aspirations. I wanted better for myself. I took the first step by admitting my life was a mess and I needed some help. It was my idea at this point, not someone trying to force their opinion on me.

On November 1, 2001, I did it, I decided to go into treatment. That was not my first time, it was my second. Because I failed the first time, I was not convinced it would work, but I went. I was willing to try something different because at that point using drugs was not working to numb the pain anymore. I wanted to learn how to address what was going on within me, and what I knew was that I could not do it alone. I needed help and at that point, I had a good understanding of where my help needed to come from. I needed a fresh start somewhere else. I ended up in Secaucus, NJ at a twenty-eight-day program. That is where I started looking within and getting honest with myself about some things. I was not trying to portray the victim in my circumstances. I needed someone who was going to assist me and give me some insight and direction.

I grew tired of trying to figure it out on my own. One of the best things I heard at the program was, I did not have to do things alone anymore. I did not have an issue with allowing someone to show me the way, I had already realized my way was not working. I went from that program to another program in Monmouth County where I stayed for six months. I learned so much about myself and the demons I was running from and dealing with. When I completed that program, I decided to stay in Monmouth County where I have now lived for twenty years.

While doing some work in the program I learned there were so many questions that would go unanswered that I wanted from my mother, but within the years of my using, my mother passed away. I had to put the pieces together the best I could and gain some acceptance of my reality. My choices brought forth my own consequences no matter how I looked at them. I became willing to accept responsibility and accountability for my actions. I had to surrender.

At twenty-six years old, I met two people who came into my life who supported and guided me, they showed me, unconditional love. They weathered the storm with me until I was ready to make the necessary changes. It was them showing up at that time in my life, and their parental guidance that led to my belief, God did hear my prayers all those years. The things I experienced did not make sense to me then, I had no understanding of why I had to go through what I did. It all makes good sense to me today. What I understand is we all go through; I believe we go through for other people. There are people in the world who can learn and benefit from our experiences. I learned to make better decisions and had a much better outcome, I never thought I would end up in such a good place in my life.

After twenty years of deliverance from drugs and alcohol, God has redeemed and restored my relationship with my sons. My daughter was born two weeks before I went into recovery, she never experienced that part of my life. Do allow me to say, every experience in my life has molded me into the awesome woman I am today. I often think back, however, I don't get stuck there anymore. It is so gratifying to be able to make healthy choices. I was the child who had no sense of direction; however, God led the way. I worked hard to achieve all my goals. I stopped looking at who didn't do what for me and focused on what I needed to do to have a better life for myself, my children, and now my grandchildren. Determined to be more than a statistic, I aimed to be the role model that I am today and I worked hard to make it happen. I am now a positive example and a reflection of hope for all to see. When I learned better, I did better.

I feel I have set the bar high within my immediate family because I want my children and grandchildren to reach for the stars. I was lost but found by God's grace and everlasting mercy. I am forever grateful for every experience I've gone through; I would not change a thing. Whenever I thought I should be somewhere other than I was, God reminded me that I was where I needed to be, and that included the good, the bad, and the ugly. I am so glad I don't look like what I've been through! I've gained acceptance with the fact that God's destiny for me is greater than my desires. (Jeremiah 29:11, NKJV)

ABOUT THE AUTHOR:
Social Media:
IG instagram.com/trulyblezzed/
FB facebook.com/sylvia.james.37
Email queenhumble2020@gmail.com

Sylvia James is a Master's Level Social Worker with pending Licensed Clinical Alcohol and Drug Counselor (LCADC). She was awarded her master's degree in Social Work from Monmouth University in Long Branch NJ and a Bachelor of Arts in Psychology from Georgian Court University in Lakewood, NJ.

James works in the substance use disorder and mental health field with fourteen years of experience working with adults with substance use and mental health disorders. As a seasoned clinician, she aims to be sensitive, empathetic, compassionate, authentic, ethical, and non-judgmental. Sylvia aspires to meet the needs of the client by meeting them where they are, using the client-centered approach, and helping them build on their strengths. After eleven years of counseling, she became an administrator. She was promoted to a supervisor position that she held for over three years. Most recently she was promoted to a directorship position.

James would like to acknowledge the women who are participating in this journey. Who thought enough of her to allow her to be a part of this amazing process. She would like to thank all of her biological children who have shown great resilience and support, her god-daughters, and daughter-in-law who have been very supportive as well. Sylvia would also like to acknowledge her godparents Charles and Deborah Raikes for loving her to life. Also, her best friend Shireen Rogers-Medley for thirty-plus years of friendship and believing in her when no one else did. Thanks again, Love you all.

"If you are not willing to learn, no one can help you. If you are determined to learn, no one can stop you."

- Zig Ziglar

FROM IMPOSSIBLE TO I'M POSSIBLE

Vallori Thomas

"Yesterday is history, tomorrow a mystery, but today is a gift. That is why it is called the present." - Unknown

It's never too late to have a happy life. It is the joy and purpose of this book. Holding on to the past, you can't grasp what's possible for you here in the present. I live my life with zest and fervor however this was not always the case. I struggled for years trying to find myself, my place, and my purpose. It seemed the more I searched the less clear I became. I was quick to take a chance on anything or anyone other than myself to avoid being left out, or seen as different, in my pursuit to belong and to be accepted. It wasn't long before I found myself in the company of people and in places, sometimes dangerous places, where I should never have been. There's no need for me to go into all the detailed unpleasantness of my past, what I want you to know is that there was a time in my life when I couldn't see the possibility of any kind. When you can't see a possibility, not only do you not know how high you can fly, you also don't know how deep you can sink.

When I finally looked up years had gone by, everything was gone: my home, my job, my family, and friends. And with them went any respect that I'd had for myself. The only thing to rival my loss of self-respect was the loss of respect that I once had for others. I had no hope and no self-esteem. I had hit bottom. And the bottom was far lower and emptier than I would have ever imagined it to be.

Frankly, the depth of the human spirit is unfathomable. A person has to plummet a great distance spiritually before she/he/they hit bottom. And you don't know where the bottom is until you hit it. That's exactly what happened to me. I found my bottom to be a cold, isolated, and lonely place. And although I felt that it wasn't a place where I could stay, and still be alive, I lingered there anyway. Indecisive. Directionless.

Life Lesson: Making no decision is still a decision made.

There are long periods in my past that I don't remember. Holiday memories that most people would cherish are not even known to me. Photographs with family and friends that might trigger a memory don't exist because of my isolation and detachment. There are huge swaths of my past from which there is no one to say, remember the time when we did "this" or "that".

Other than being sick and tired, I wish that I could tell you exactly what happened to spark the turnaround, but I can't. I don't know if it was something that someone said to me or something that I read on a billboard or something that my inner voice whispered. I only know that there came a divine moment when I knew that the direction that I should move in was up –up from my bottom. It hit me that the same intensity of focus and energy that got me to my bottom, I could use that same intensity of focus and energy to pursue what I genuinely wanted, so I did. It was then that I first began to consider my life and myself as a real possibility.

Slowly, I began to rebuild my life, piece by piece. The spiritual void within me was so great, though, that I could only measure my growth in things like wearing clean clothes that fit; sleeping in the same bed under the same roof every night; and looking people in the eye and speaking to them without using razor-sharp expletives.

One day, after being unemployed for God only knows how long, I found a job, and for the first time in a long time, I embraced the opportunity to develop substantive relationships. I felt that I had finally reconnected with humanity.

"The only way for human beings to experience themselves as being human, in my view, is in relationship with other human beings."

I soon discovered that I was pretty good at being human. (Who knew?) People seemed to enjoy being around me and one day during an ordinary conversation with coworkers about nothing in particular, "just stuff," a colleague asked, "What do you really want?" The question stunned me. I was stupefied. I couldn't answer. I don't think anyone had ever actually asked me that question that way. What did I want?

I can only imagine what I must have looked like to my coworkers at that moment when, as the resident "Chatty Kathy," I wasn't being quite so chatty. It was a simple enough question, and yet it was so potent that it stopped me in my tracks. What did I want? I didn't quite know the answer, but the question itself had me think of myself in a way that shifted everything!

Years later, in the methodical rebuilding of my life, I would come to understand how pivotal that question was. I started focusing my thoughts and energy toward having my dreams and the life I wanted, and that changed everything! I could finally see possibility in myself that I couldn't see before. It was crystal clear that my life and my happiness were all up to me!

"There's nothing like bearing witness to the fragility and resiliency of the human spirit, especially when it's your own."

I realized I had been in a "holding pattern". Looking back, it was like I was waiting for my circumstances to give me the permission to be happy, to do what was important to me. Until it hit me. All the reasons I had made up as "why not" weren't even reasons, they were mere excuses.

I started speaking about my ideas and desires as if they mattered. As a result, the people in my life began interacting with me as though they mattered too; more importantly, I got it. I mattered!

I surrounded myself with like-minded people. Those who base success on principles and values rather than possessions and titles. With support from mentors and my network, I was able to see the vastness of possibility ahead of me. And see the impact of having choices from an empowered perspective.

Life Lesson: The thing about possibility is, the more you apply it the more there is. You are far more resilient than you know.

Resilience allows you, me, and anyone else to come back stronger than ever before. Resilience is about overcoming. It is about human resolve, and the ability to "rise from the ashes," so to speak. Resilient people see failure and setbacks as learning curves that empowers them to change course and soldier on. The first time that I looked back on how I was able to rebuild my life, I discovered that I was far more resilient than I could have imagined. I was able not only to bounce back but bounce forward. It is in bouncing forward that I got my "legs" to move toward and live the life I desired.

How resilient are you right now? I can assure you that, regardless of your answer you are exponentially more resilient than you think you are, and you will succeed in ways that you cannot even imagine right now! I know this to be true because it is said:

"A Champion is one who gets up when they shouldn't." -Jack Dempsey

Clearly, you and I are still standing!

It starts with saying YES! When you say "yes" to yourself you choose to lead your life. To truly take responsibility for it, to take charge, to take control – you are choosing a life of possibility. You discover that you have more peace, more truth, more time, more joy, more success, and more happiness. When you choose to lead your life rather than life leading you, you experience a life full of more than you ever thought was possible.

If you take nothing else from what you've read, remember this; You don't have to be amazing to start, you just have to start to be amazing!

Today is a great day to be AMAZING!

ABOUT THE AUTHOR:
Social Media:
IG @wowcoachv/@wowtalk2021
FB Vallori Thomas
Website Address www.vallorithomas.com
Email Vallori@vallorithomas.com

Vallori Thomas, 2021 WeInspire Ambassador, is an accredited member of Forbes Coaches Council, an ICF-certified Coach, the Founder of The Institute at WOW Coaching and Consulting, and the author of "POSSIBILITOLOGY: *It's A Great Day to Be Amazing*". Her book is a primer on a life perspective that brought her back into the mainstream of life from an isolated marginal existence.

Thomas went on to become an executive at a prominent fashion house, founded a nonprofit to empower women, and established "WOW Coaching & Consulting" to share with others what life has taught her about overcoming, thriving, and the divine gift of reinventing oneself. She facilitates corporate training as well as adult and executive leadership development programs and has delivered women's empowerment training for Harvard University Graduate Students.

Vallori is a practitioner of Context Mastery with more than a decade of experience in team/group dynamics, communication, and both one-to-one and group coaching, her expertise encompasses process improvement, vision-building, and breakthrough learning.

Services offered:
- Personal and Professional Development Expert
- DEI Trainer
- Facilitator/Leadership Trainer
- Keynote Speaker
- Certified Executive Coach

VISIBLY INVISIBLE

Electra Fowler-Willis

"I rarely felt heard or seen. My small voice saying, hey, here I am, don't you see me? I'M RIGHT HERE! I like to draw and watch scary movies, I like dancing and listening to different types of music, I love reading a good book, I am a little clumsy and awkward at times…Oh, and I love chocolate. Hey, here I am. Don't you see me? I'm right here."

Visibly invisible, from as far back as I can remember I wore this feeling like an ill-fitted hat that stayed in place. Regardless of the direction in which I turned it never fell off.

I felt out of place, bypassed, and overlooked.

As I attempt to share myself with you, I am trying desperately to remember when these feelings began. However, the harder I try the more elusive the memory becomes. Then I realize my inner child continues to be the gatekeeper of all things painful and uncomfortable. I am grateful for her, and I have come to love, respect, and cherish her. She weathered some mighty storms that kept me safe and allowed me to be here today to share my story with you.

Moreover, as I sit at the precipice of my second decade in recovery, I can let her know that it is all right. I can handle it now.

I want to say that feeling began when I learned a dark-skinned girl was less than desirable. Convinced that I would have to be someone "extra-ordinary" to feel worthy.

All those empowering hashtags that we see today like, "black girl magic," "my black is beautiful," or "Melanin Poppin'" were not popular yet. Instead, I heard things like you are pretty to be so dark-skinned. Which for me translated to, "I see you, but I do not see you."

Then again, I want to say that it was the strained and unpredictable relationship I had with my father who struggled with alcoholism. The only time I felt he saw me was when I did something that would result in punishment. I'd get in trouble for the "entire" summer regardless of the season of the offense.

Perhaps it was the summers-when I was not on punishment-that I spent at my cousin's house. They were older than me and I looked at them like the big sisters that I never had. I was shy and quiet around them growing up, and I admired them both a lot. They had such big personalities, unlike me, who was told that I acted and spoke too properly. Which again in my mind translated to, "We see you, but we do not see you."

So, here I am this young black girl. Just trying to navigate the unintentional implicit biases of those who would influence me and bring meaning into my world.

Truthfully, I cannot tell you the exact moment that this feeling took hold. I just know that it did and that it would be the driving force throughout my adolescent, teenage and young adult years. The velocity at which my life would spiral out of control was devastating.

By the time I was twenty years old I was grist for the mill, and substances became my escape, they made me visible. For the next eleven years, my life became a dismal pantomime, as I revolved through the legal system, and rehabilitation centers.

Glimpses of that little girl who liked to draw, and dance to the songs she played on her Winnie-the-pooh record player hung in the distance. In her place stood a faceless woman with a plethora of masks, ready to be whomever someone needed her to be. Confused, hurt, fractured, and lost, I truly was visibly invisible.

August 11, 2001, would change my life forever. One night, lost in my thoughts and wandering aimlessly because by now my life had no direction. The police stopped me for trespassing on a vacant lot. They asked for the usual information which resulted in my arrest for unpaid fines. Although I was void of spirit and purpose the tiny spark of hope that I managed to hold onto would turn into a wellspring of possibility.

In past attempts at recovery, it was the pain of one consequence after another that drove me to seek help. Conversely, the shame and guilt of those consequences would drive me right back out the door.

Something was different this time. As I surveyed my surroundings and took note of the other faceless people, I knew it was over. After three months I was released. New possibilities abounding I was ready to face this thing called life head-on.

Early recovery was a cascade of changing landscapes, as I embarked on my journey toward self-improvement. I began working through the trauma of being an adult child of an alcoholic. I began working through self-hatred. Dreams and goals that had fallen into the abyss of my despair began to materialize. I was learning to live and accept life as it showed up. I learned to be a mother to my children, a daughter to my mother, and a friend to my girls who never gave up on me. Through it all, I was still standing.

Now, when it came to relationships, I was clueless. I had no idea what a healthy relationship looked like. If he said I love you, in the immortal words of the late great Marvin Gaye I said, "let's get it on, ah, baby, let's get it on." Sadly, I was a classic example of that little girl searching for love.

It was not until one of the women who would share space in my life as a sponsor, mentor, and friend told me I needed to take time to get to know myself. That I needed to develop the very qualities that I wanted in a partner.

She 'suggested' that I date myself. Tired of dead-end relationships, with nine years in recovery, I took the suggestion. This was a game-changer. I treated myself well, and I began to enjoy the time I spent alone.

An equally pivotal moment in my recovery was when I was unceremoniously told, "Damn E make a decision." This statement would prove to be one of the most impactful things said to me.

With trepidation, I tested the waters. My decisions were filled with fear and uncertainty. Nevertheless, I pressed on trying out this new superpower. I made some good and some not-so-good decisions. Miraculously, the longer I stayed on this journey the stronger my foundation became. The broader my base grew, and the higher my point of freedom extended, my decisions became healthier and healthier.

One of the greatest decisions I made was to gain a relationship with God for myself. He is my Savior and my redeemer. It is deeply personal. He has blessed me with a loving and supportive husband to whom I married nine years ago. I have relationships with my children, a career I am passionate about, and a phenomenal network of women in my life. It bears repeating that as I sit at the precipice of twenty years in recovery, I am so grateful that "through it all, I'm still standing".

~Untitled~

Lost dreams;
Goals;
Aspirations;
Trapped in someone else's mental snapshot of who I was;
First unwilling than unable to escape this alternate reality;
NEVER, truly knowing, loving, embracing me!
Like a mime behind an invisible wall, walking toward an invisible fall
Looking for the flying traipse;
Gasping in the stifling breeze;
FIGHTING, FIGHTING, to be free…
NEVER, truly knowing, loving, embracing me!
Locked in my mind starts to spin;
Who is this I see; This stranger pretending to be me
Living in my space, my essence;
She didn't know she ALWAYS had a presence
WELL, I want me back, my smile, my strut, my sway…
You see my plans were never to give her away,
She is beautiful, unique, bold, creative, intelligent, caring, compassionate, funny, insightful, confident, competent, strong, empowered, she is COURAGEOUS…
Fear no longer lives here….
My price was high, I paid the ultimate fee…I gave away my freedom to be free;
FINALLY, I have come to know, love, and embrace me!

- Electra Fowler-Willis

I would like to acknowledge my husband who keeps me encouraged with every endeavor I embark upon. My mother for just being an awesome woman of God.

My resilient children whom I love more than words can say.

And to all the phenomenal women who laid their story out in these pages.

ABOUT THE AUTHOR:
Social Media:
LI linkedin.com/in/electra-fowler-willis-8964b43b/
FB facebook.com/electra.fowler
Email efowler123@gmail.com

Electra is a Master-level Clinician who has worked in the field of counseling since 2013. She is a Licensed Social Worker (LSW) and a Licensed Clinical Alcohol and Drug Counselor (LCADC). Fowler obtained her master's degree in Social Work from Monmouth University and her bachelor's degree in Business Management from New Jersey City University.

Electra has worked tirelessly in the helping field. Her philosophy and passion for serving others made her transition from a fifteen-year career in healthcare to social work seamless. Fowler-Willis is a member of Good Hope Baptist Church in Asbury Park NJ, where she has worked with members of her congregation to bring awareness to the necessity of outreach and building kinship to heal marginalized communities.

Electra believes in focusing on interventions and preventative measures, that will aid in assisting individuals that struggle in various areas of their lives, find workable solutions, that will allow them to live to their fullest potential. She is currently employed as a Primary Therapist at Recovery Centers of America in South Amboy, NJ. Additionally, Fowler-Willis works as a psychotherapist providing individual therapy at Mind Your Mind mental health services in Hamilton, NJ. She has been a proud member of Zeta Phi Beta Sorority Inc. since 2017.

Electra and her husband Tyrone currently reside in Neptune NJ. Their blended family consists of five children and one grandchild.

BLESSED BEYOND MEASURE

Debra McKinney-Hill

I was born on April 9, 1959, in Charleston, South Carolina to a nineteen-year-old single mother who already had three other children. All four of us had different fathers, none of whom were in our lives. I could only imagine the fear felt by our mother being a single mom with no help at that age. Her childhood was during the racial segregation in the Jim Crow era. Her father was a raging alcoholic and her mother experienced abuse by him in every imaginable way possible. My grandmother fled the south running away from my grandfather because she could no longer deal with the abuse. My grandmother would eventually settle in Paterson, New Jersey seeking refuge.

Not long after, my mother along with her four children followed suit and settled there as well. Upon arriving in the new state, we stayed with my grandmother for a little while until my mother met a man who she would later marry. Together they had six children bringing a total of ten kids living in the house. I was about three years old when my stepfather came into my life. I was a happy-go-lucky child. I enjoyed playing with my siblings. We played games like hopscotch, double Dutch, hide and seek, shooting marbles, one two three red-light, dodge ball, freeze, and so many others. I enjoyed putting puzzles together, riding my bike, sewing, and making cakes with my easy bake oven.

All of that changed when my stepfather began touching me inappropriately in the private parts of my body. I was ten years old when this abuse began to happen. Knowing and feeling that this was wrong, I immediately told my mother when she came home from gambling that night. However, my stepfather told my mother that he didn't do anything. What kind of monster knowingly does the things he did to innocent children? They labeled me a liar, a hard-headed child, a trouble maker, and manipulated me into thinking that I was bad and this was my fault. My stepfather even said that I was making up stories because I didn't like discipline when my mother was out gambling, which she did often.

As the abuse continued, I went from a sweet innocent little girl to one that became angry, bitter, and confused. I began suffering in disbelief and crying aloud for help from the inner turmoil that created pain in my eyes. I was screaming out to any adult that would listen, my grandmother, my uncle, and my aunt.

They said, "It is none of our business what is happening at your momma's house. We cannot tell her what to do."

My uncle even said, "I'm not messing with your momma; your momma beats up men."

From that point on for the next five years with no help in sight, my behavior began to change. My perspective about life differed so much. I began to hate everyone. I started wilding out with boys. I would go to school and pick fights with somebody every day. I'd stomp them and bang their heads to the ground. I even sat behind a girl in my class with long hair down to her butt and cut her hair off with scissors. Well, I got the beating of a lifetime when I got home. My mother told me she was going to beat the black off me and tear my ass out of the frame.

Because of the ongoing punishment I received, I wanted to kill my stepfather, my mother, and all of the other adults that stood by and did nothing. I started thinking of ways to commit this act telling no one of my plans. Of course, I did not follow through with it. However, I still could not sleep. Every time I closed my eyes, I would see my stepfather abusing me. The trauma messed up my mind. I was an emotional wreck.

When I got to high school, I tried to take my mind off things by getting involved in sports and other activities. I started playing softball, I ran track, I was a majorette, and I did some acting but nothing would take the place of the emptiness I felt inside.

I would come in the house and say, hi to my mother and then turn to my stepfather and say, "What's up MF?" I wanted him to feel the pain that I was still experiencing. I did not care about him at all and I wanted him to know it. I wondered how he was able to keep lying to my mother about his shenanigans and get away with it. How could she believe him and not me? I was only a child. I absolutely loved my mother. But it pained me to see him when I would visit her. You see I always felt like she should have left him, especially when years later she found out I was telling the truth.

This truth came out when I was fifteen. They expected me to carry on like nothing ever happened. For me, the damage was already done. All I could think about was all of the beatings I endured because of the lies my stepfather told about me. I just could not get all of the horrible visions out of my head. Never having the privilege to experience real love, I started listening to teenage boys whispering sweet nothings in my ear. I ended up having a baby in high school. My daughter's father was not happy about the pregnancy and ended up being an absent father in her life. My self-esteem was at an all-time low. Honestly, it was under the basement. I had no idea who I was, this little girl lost in a big world. I was a baby with a baby. Because I did not know my identity, I ended up in an abusive relationship for the next thirteen years with someone who sold and used drugs.

With the hand dealt to me, I tried to live life as normal as possible but I soon realized I was just existing and not living. I was walking through life wounded. Without an outlet such as therapy or having a relationship with a God, I began getting high. When I started using drugs, they took the pain away and numbed my mind. I used heroin, cocaine, pills, weed and drank various kinds of alcohol. I never said I wanted to be a drug addict when I grew up. But when I got introduced to them, I thought I had found a solution to all of my problems because I didn't have to feel anymore. I secretly got high on weekends for a year, after that, it was all downhill. At first, I was able to hold down a job, pay my bills, and take care of my daughter.

Before I knew it, I was strung out. My life became quickly unmanageable. For the next several years, I went from being a nice responsible young lady to not being present for my daughter. I was physically there for a while but not present. I was no longer able to show up for work without being high. I did whatever I needed to do to get high again and again and again, I got high every day all day. I committed various crimes. I sold drugs. I also committed strong-arm robberies, breaking and entering, assault, and selling my body. It had gotten so bad that every time I turned around, I was in and out of jail in damn near every city I went to. Besides jail, other consequences were homelessness, lost jobs, and broken relationships with friends and family members.

I had adapted to the ways of the streets and the drug culture which meant anything goes. I put myself in so many dangerous situations. I would go up on the roof of the projects in NY to get high all by myself. I found myself wandering around many different streets in the city. Morningside Ave, 116th street, 178 street, 2nd Ave, and 139 street to name a few. I also ran the streets of Paterson, Trenton, Plainfield, Passaic, and many others. More often than not I got high by myself wherever I went. On occasion, I did get high with other people but because of my sexual abuse, I withdrew from life and became a loner.

Although I chose to get high, I didn't know how I ended up being where I was. It was very difficult for me to believe that this was my life, I felt caught up in a vicious cycle. Unbeknownst to me, God was there the whole time and he was orchestrating a path for my deliverance. Strange things began to happen to me amid my madness. Internally, I kept saying to myself I want to go to rehab, but I didn't know what one was. I wondered, who put that word in my thoughts and in my mouth? I had no clue. The people I was getting high with began saying to me I looked like I didn't belong out there with them using drugs. Of course, I tried to prove them wrong by getting that much higher.

One of the few bosses I had told me he knew something was wrong with me but he didn't know what and that I should go to church to get help. I told him there was nothing wrong with me and I am not going to anybody's church. On another occasion, while at the soup kitchen a woman pulled me out of the line and said she sees something in me that I didn't see in myself. I said lady please leave me alone, I just came here to get something to eat. She continued speaking to me and said you need to go to rehab and if I agreed to go, she would give me the bus money to get there. Of course, I said sure just to get the money so that I could buy more drugs. At that time, I had no intentions of going to anyone's rehab.

Another time I was on my way to pick up some money in a new town. A car that I did not recognize passed by me and backed up, it was my sister. She asked me what was I doing over there and where was I going. I lied and told her that I had not eaten for days so she could give me some money. She told me to get in the car and took me to Gino's offering to buy the food. That was not what I wanted her to do but I got in the car anyway. To my surprise and her reluctance, she handed me a $20 bill for me to get something to eat later as well. She volunteered to give me a ride but I declined. Before she pulled off, she begged me and made me promise not to buy drugs with the money she gave me. I said ok but I was not able to keep that promise. As soon as she left, I went right to the drug dealer to buy more drugs.

Later, that night I called my grandmother, fake crying. I told her the same lie thinking that I would be able to get some money out of her but she told me to hold on one minute she had something for me. Well, she came back to the phone and said here is the number to the rehab that helped your cousin get his life together maybe they can help you too. She told me she loved me and made me promise that I would call the place. As angry as I was, I did not want to let my grandmother down so I made the call. The facility scheduled a date and time for me to come into treatment. The day before I was to go in, as any good drug addict would, I wanted to get that last high and walked into a sting and got arrested.

The arresting officer was the brother of two sisters I had run track and played softball with. Because I knew the family, I thought I was going to get over and I begged him to let me go. Thankfully, he did not and told me that I needed a rest. He said what would your family members say if they saw how bad you look? He preceded to tell me that he knew I could do better and he was going to do what he felt was in my best interest, arrest me.

Fortunately for me, I went in front of the judge that same day. But because of my record, the judge said he was going to send me to jail for a long time. I told the judge my scheduled rehab stay was the next day but he didn't believe me. In fact, he said he has heard it all before. He said all addicts lie to get their way. I said your honor if you let me make a phone call, I could verify what I'm saying. He said no. We are not going to waste time with your attempt to manipulate this court. You are going to jail and that is going to be the end of it. I was pleading with him to let me make the call because this time I was telling the truth.

Out of nowhere, the stenographer spoke up and said, "Your honor, I will make the call for her, that way if she is lying you could sentence her to jail right now."

The judge said although he already knew what the outcome of the call would be, he would allow her to make the call.

After about ten minutes she returned to the courtroom and said "Your honor, she wasn't lying, her rehab stay starts tomorrow."

The judge turned to me and said, "You must have an angel watching over you. But if for any reason you do not go to the rehab and come back in my courtroom, I will definitely throw the book at you and put you underneath the jail."

I knew in my heart that I had come to the end of my road. I was stuck in a place for so long that I did not know how to get out of it. Without question, I had hit rock bottom.

That was the beginning of my end. You see I believe God orchestrated all those situations to happen as he was preparing the way to bring me out of the darkness into his marvelous light. Against my better judgment, I did return to the block to buy drugs after my release from jail that night, but I surrendered and went to rehab the next day which was September 8, 1994. I was finally ready to give up my old ways and learn how to live a life free from drugs and alcohol and the trauma of my past. However, due to the massive amounts of heroin I was using every day, I had difficulty with severe withdrawal in the first two weeks of the program. I could not do much of anything. I could not eat or sleep and I was throwing up everywhere. I was sick as a dog and had no energy at all. I would stand in the shower under the hottest water I could stand several times a day just so I could feel better momentarily.

Going into the third week of the program my body began to repair itself from all of the wear and tear I had subjected it to. Drugs turned me into someone I did not want to be and I wouldn't wish this hell on my worst enemy. While in treatment, God blessed me with one of his servants as my counselor. In our sessions, he would talk about a loving God who cared about me and wanted the best for me. His discussions about this God piqued my interest and I began to embrace it slowly but surely. As my mind opened, I started to hunger and thirst like a deer panting by the rivers of water for more of God's loving presence in my life. My counselor allowed me to go to church with one of the senior sisters of the program.

While at the service I experienced an overwhelming feeling of warmth come over me as the word went forth that I had never felt before. I could not explain the feeling if I tried, but I knew I wanted to explore and find out what it was. Unfortunately, the woman graduated and moved back home to another county. I wasn't able to go back to church the rest of the time there, but I felt like a power source was drawing me closer to him.

When I completed the program eleven months later and still holding on to my experience, I started visiting different churches. In meetings, I'd share about this powerful source that was pulling me and how the intensity would not go away. I felt there was more to my recovery than just attending Narcotics Anonymous meetings. God was gracious enough to put people in my path who knew what I was talking about. Once the meeting was over two different gentlemen came up to me and invited me to church. I did not go right away but after some persistence by one of them, I went. As I listened to the sermons delivered, it appeared as if God was talking directly to me. I felt the same warmth that I had experienced at the other church a year prior. I felt a peace that I had never experienced. This was the missing piece of my life. So, I joined the church and have been there ever since.

I learned that God loved me my whole life and he was patiently waiting for me to open the door to my heart and allow him to come in. God let me know that he had chosen me and he knew me before I was in my mother's womb. He knew the plans he had for me. God knew that I would go through everything that I had gone through for His glory. I have learned that my brokenness can minister to others about the goodness of the Lord. Now I know that it was good that have been afflicted because it was my path to the Almighty Savior, Jesus Christ. There's nothing like God telling you to live and not die. I discovered that God did not bring me this far to let me fall by the wayside. He brought me out of the perils of drug addiction, rejection, and hopelessness. He rescued me from depression, molestation, physical, mental, spiritual, and emotional abuse.

Sometimes life doesn't always go the way we think it should. I have endured various trials in my recovery where the thought of using drugs again didn't seem like a bad idea. Things were going quite well in our lives. My husband and I bought a nice house together. Our children were doing good and out of nowhere my husband got diagnosed with cancer which he succumbed to eight months later. Before his diagnosis, I had suffered one loss after another. My mother, my grandmother, a few of my uncles, my first love, my spiritual father, and three of my best friends were all gone home to be with the Lord. However, the death of my husband at the age of fifty-two was incomprehensible for me. It was so sudden that the grief I experienced knocked me off course.

I was numb for such a long time. My faith wavered on and off. I felt helpless, hopeless, hurt, devastated, and angry at God. I went into immediate shock and disbelief. I thought that I was losing my mind. I was heartbroken. I couldn't breathe, think, or move. Now that I knew God, I was waiting for Him to perform a miracle as only he can. He did it before. But not this time. More often than not I wanted to give up because I thought God had let us down. I had never experienced such an overwhelming feeling of grief and loss. Although I had lost loved ones before and knew that death was a part of life, my husband's death left me paralyzed for years.

I could not understand the reason I had such a response. Everything I thought was going to happen did not. I thought my husband's healing was going to be on this side. But God! Despite all of the things I had gone through—God had my best interest at heart. As I honestly told God about my pain, my feelings, and all of the hurt, God allowed me to focus on his never-ending love. God whispered in my ear and assured me that he was with me and my husband every step of the way. He told me that absence from the body is to be present with the Lord and that my husband was resting in his bosom. His healing was in heaven. God reminded me that he is the God of the living and those that believe in him shall never die. There will be a time when I will be with my husband and my loved ones once again. We will never experience the pain of separation.

Although my journey was not easy, I have survived my traumatic childhood. I decided to take control over my life and do something different other than be a casualty of the streets. I vowed never to use drugs again or go back to jail. I've often asked myself. Why would God allow me to go through so much pain, suffering, and heartache? The Bible says in this world we will have trouble and we will suffer for Christ's sake. So, I soon discovered that suffering has played a huge role in my growing experience. God ultimately created a shift in the atmosphere in my life. He delivered me from the depths of shame to the heights of His love and His glory. He has graced me to deal with whatever hardships come my way. New opportunities arose out of my pain and allowed me to rise above the ashes. Doors began to open for me to utilize my experience. I have been charged to carry the message of hope to the brokenhearted and to help them overcome any addiction issues; so, they could see themselves as God sees them.

God afforded me the opportunity to further my education which allowed me to go to college to obtain several degrees. I have a master's degree in pastoral counseling with a concentration in addiction and recovery. I am a licensed certified drug and alcohol counselor. I am the CEO of Overflow Ministries which reaches out to the community. God has gifted me with talents and abilities to make a difference. I have dedicated my life to giving back. Today I know without a shadow of a doubt that I am walking in alignment with the divine destiny God called me to walk in. I know that it is Christ alone who empowers me to keep standing. I am more than a conqueror thru Jesus Christ. I am on a transformational journey of self-discovery, truth, and healing as I continue to press toward the mark and mission designed for me. God called me to prosper.

As I continue to rejoice in my deliverance, I will be celebrating twenty-seven years free from active addiction on September 9,

2021. When I look back over my life and see how God has brought me through, I give thanks for the good, the bad, the ugly, and the indifferent. I express gratitude for the strength to persevere. I have value. I have meaning. I have a purpose. I am courageous. I am unstoppable. I am determined. I am successful. I am favored. Most of all I am who God says I am. I am His masterpiece. My purpose still stands because my best days are yet to come.

"If you are always trying to be normal you will never know how amazing you can be."

- Maya Angelou

ABOUT THE AUTHOR:
Social Media:
IG @debrod2.dmkh
FB debrod2.dmkh
Website Address debramckinneyhill.com
Email debrod2.dmkh@gmail.com

Debra Mc Kinney-Hill is a #1 Amazon bestselling author and is currently working on her next book. Debra was born in Charleston, SC, and raised in Paterson NJ. She is a loving mother and grandmother to Shakia Mc Kinney and Imoni Brooks. Debra has more than twenty years of experience in treating addiction and mental illness and she brings with her a wealth of knowledge.

Debra holds a master's degree in Pastoral Counseling: Addictions and Recovery from Liberty University. She is also a Licensed Clinical Alcohol and Drug Counselor, a Human Service Board Certified Practitioner, and she teaches Sunday School to adult new members. Debra is the founder of Overflow Ministries, whose mission is to serve the needs of the people in the community.

She has a very welcoming and helpful approach when dealing with folks from all walks of life. She desires to empower them to tap into the strength they possess inside and to provide them with the necessary resources. More than anything, Debra is grateful to God for using her heartaches and brokenness for His glory.

Services offered:
- Counseling
- Spiritual Life Coach
- Motivational Speaker

CHOICES

Robin Langhorne

I remember the first time I "Got it." Back then they called it "freebase." I was in NYC with the then love of my life. He dabbled in drugs. Nothing big time but he had some connections. I thought we were there for weed and some blow (coke). We were waiting in the living room of a low-lit apartment. There were a few people ahead of us, and he was the type of person who talked with everybody, a real people person. That's what I loved about him.

We had been sitting there for a while, and finally, they called him in the backroom. I didn't go with him. I waited on the couch. Some time had gone by and I was getting a little uncomfortable. Nobody was chattin' it up anymore. I kicked into my "never let 'em see you sweat" mode. I was in NYC! In a drug dealer's apartment. I knew people in Asbury Park that dealt drugs, but this was different. Unfamiliar. I didn't know where I was or how we got there. I couldn't leave. I was totally dependent on the man in the other room. I didn't know what was on the other side of the apartment door if I did decide to leave. Will someone rape me? Rob me? Or both? So, I sat there. An hour went by, no Boo.

Going into the second hour he came out with a big smile on his face (oh how that smile would make me melt) You alright? (My mind, No!!!) my mouth Yes. Good, good. It's going to be a few more minutes. He gave me some reason I can't remember and a kiss and disappeared back into the other room. So, I explained to myself that this was the way you supported your man. Drug dealer or not you stand by him and support him. You don't let the others in the room know you have a problem with what's happening. So, I sat there, watching TV, and not interested in what was playing. Too paranoid to ask if we could change the channel. Just act comfortable!

This scenario went on several times. He'd come out, ask if I was ok, and say it would be a few more minutes. Then eventually, he came out and asked me to come in the back with him. I don't exactly remember how it happened right now but he offered me something in a glass pipe.

Now in my time I've smoked hash and weed from a glass pipe, we called it a bong, so this is what I thought I was doing. Only this stuff was melting, and I could see the smoke curl up in the bowl of the glass.

Everyone looked at me, "Did you get it?"

I replied, "No."

He lit it again, "Did you get it now?"

I lied and said, "Yeah."

What was I supposed to get? They knew I was lying. I didn't get another chance to "get it." They didn't waste their time with me wasting whatever it was that we were doing.

Shortly after, we left the apartment in Brooklyn and headed back to Jersey. I don't remember asking him what just happened. But what I do remember is the progression of him in the drug game and occasional encounters with him smoking from a glass pipe. I don't recall him ever doing it in my presence. But you could tell something was off.

One particular day he brought the pipe to me and told me no matter what he said do not give him that pipe. I didn't know why he didn't just throw it away but I did as he asked and I took the pipe and hid it. I don't need to tell you he begged me relentlessly to give him the pipe back. I said no but he wouldn't take no for an answer. It got so bad I got the pipe from its hiding place and smashed it on the dresser in front of him. He was like, oh wow, with a shocked look on his face.

He said, "Thanks, Rob I needed that. I'm glad you did that."

But little did I know that it was the beginning of the end of our relationship. I went all downhill from there. He was never happy with me anymore. He complained a lot about the things he used to love about me.

Soon after he asked me to move out. This was after an argument we had. I brushed it off attributing it to the heat of the moment. A few weeks later he said it again but I still didn't believe that's what he wanted. We had just had a little girl. One that we had planned. This was no, "oops" baby. Did I mention he had given me a promise ring? I also had a six-year-old that thought of him as her father. Where was I going at the drop of a hat?

One day he let me know he meant business. I had to leave and he didn't seem to care how that happened. It devastated me. Luckily, my dad came to the rescue. He moved me into his parents' house that they left for him. I cried for days. When we spoke again, he told me things were moving too fast. He needed some time to himself. And you know what? I believed him. I would let him come over and spend the night as well as me doing the same. Hoping that we would work it out.

I went up North one evening, to meet my sis and some of her friends at a Club. Mr. V's I think it was. I had an awesome time. On the way home, a little voice said go by your Boo's house and surprise him. I listened to the little voice and headed that way listening to music on the WBLS' Quiet Storm. It put me in the mood for love.

I went around back because that door was always open. When I went to open the door, he was there. Reeking of some other

I can't remember when things started to change but during marriage counseling sessions we were arguing in the pastor's office. It went from being all about me to, "Why everything got to be about you?" I attributed it to cold feet. We had just purchased a house together and were getting married all in the same year. "He's just got pre-marital jitters". Do you notice how I continue to make excuses for bad behavior? That was my m.o. It kept me in denial. It kept me from making an uncomfortable decision.

I continued to make wedding plans. I'm finally going to get it right I would think. I had so many relationships and just gave the milk away. Now I had an opportunity to get it right and not feel guilty when I lay down at night.

My mother was so excited that she was helping her daughter plan her wedding. We picked out colors, favors, sent out invitations, went shopping for bridesmaid dresses, and chose fabric for my wedding dress. Instead of being an exciting time she witnessed my pain.

One of those times she asked, "Are you sure you want to get married?" By then we were about 80% into the process with invites sent out, so how could I change my mind now?

Boy, do I now wish that I had dared to say "No." It could have saved me a lot of heartache and pain. We didn't last six months. He was in and out of the house and our marriage. While in our home group he announced that he wanted a divorce. That was how I found out. I found out he wanted a divorce along with everyone else. Devastated I wanted to slide up under my chair and crawl out of the room. My sponsor looked at me and knew I was about to burst. She took me outside and I just broke down.

That started another painful series of events. Those feelings were so familiar. Much like when the previous relationship abruptly ended. The rejection and broken promise were too much to bear. I felt like I was going to die. You know they use the metaphor of a broken heart. Let me tell you a broken heart is real. Just like breaking a bone, a broken heart is a painful thing. There is a resetting that must take place. This time I didn't turn to something to help me escape. I had a foundation of men and women who were there to support me through it. One day at a time. They told me I would survive my emotions and I did. The grieving process was full of a lot of back-and-forth feelings of shock, denial, guilt, anger, bargaining, and depression. Not necessarily in that order. I vacillated between all of them until finally, I came to a point of acceptance. I can't tell you when it happened but one day I woke up and realized that I wasn't talking about that chapter of my life anymore. I had turned the page.

I realized that I had been giving my power away. The power I found had been with me all the time. I just had to stop resisting and accept it, the power of God. When I started to work on that relationship all things changed. That didn't mean I didn't want to marry again. It just meant that I didn't have to marry. I had learned to be happy in my own company. Learn how to date me. Show me what I wanted and needed. Learn my worth. Because if I don't love myself, how can I expect someone else to love me? Since that time, I have stopped putting my dreams on hold. I have stepped out on faith and started that coffee business that I had been dreaming about. For the last three years, RoBeans has been a familiar part of the Asbury Park community and the surrounding areas. I am on the local business committee and have formed relationships with individuals that want to help my business grow. The possibilities have been endless. I love what I am doing. They say if you love what you do, you'll never work a day in your life.

I eventually married a wonderful man who adores me and I adore him. One who supports me in my endeavors and is truly my best friend. We talk about any and everything. He is my life partner. God brought us together at the right time. I don't allow our union to get in the way of my relationship with God. I have found that to be the most important connection. And because of that, I am still standing.

ABOUT THE AUTHOR:
Social Media:
IG instagram.com/RobeansBeans
FB facebook.com/RobeansBeans
Website Address https://www.therobeanery.com/
Email robeansbeans@gmail.com

Mrs. Langhorne is the owner of RoBeans LLC, a mobile coffee and dessert truck. She is known as the mobile barista along with her daughter E'Niah and son Richard. Robin has started the young entrepreneur's ministry in the "Christian Cafe" at The Rebirth Church where she is on the board of trustees.

Mrs. Langhorne has been a licensed respiratory practitioner for over twenty years. In 2020 she was a part of a team of professionals that saved dozens of lives during the pandemic. She continues her work as a full-time respiratory therapist at Specialty Hospital of Central NJ.

Robin has been an active part of the community and participates as a member of the Asbury Park business committee.

Newly married, Robin resides in Ocean County, New Jersey with her husband Rudy Langhorne. They have a blended family of eleven children, fourteen grandchildren, and six great-grandchildren.

ABOUT THE LEAD AUTHOR

Ms. Hostler is a Master-level Clinician and has worked in the counseling field for over twenty years. She is a Licensed Evangelist in the Church of God and Christ, a Licensed Clinical Mental Health Counselor (LCMHC), a Licensed Clinical Addiction Specialist (LCAS), and a National Certified Counselor (NCC). She obtained her second master's degree from North Carolina Central University in Clinical Mental Health. Ms. Hostler's first master's degree is in Psychological Counseling from Monmouth University (Long Branch, NJ). She obtained her Bachelor of Science from Thomas Edison University in Trenton, NJ.

Judith is passionate about her work as it relates to helping individuals overcome obstacles that hinder their emotional, physical, and personal growth. She finds immense pleasure in watching individuals use skills learned through counseling, coaching, and ministry as a tool to find or recover skills and personal strengths that lead to a joyful and triumphant life. Ms. Hostler's career path has been directed toward gender-responsive care with a focus on trauma-informed care. She is currently employed at the Alcohol Drug Council of NC as the Coordinator of Perinatal Substance Project; she also provides counseling at DeNome Alliance Counseling Center where she operates as a consultant. Judith also serves on the Executive Leadership team as the Co-

Director of Member services at Victorious Praise Fellowship in Durham, NC

Judith currently resides in North Carolina with the love of her life, her husband, Elder Robert Hostler. They have a blended family, seven children, and eleven grand loves. Her mission is to be the conduit that helps those she counsel understand and internalize that they are enough.

Social Media:
IG instagram.com/judejj65/
FB facebook.com/jude.johnsonhostler
Website Address https://denomealliances.com/
Email journeytohigherheights@gmail.com

Services offered:
Therapy, coaching, public speaking, conference planning, and retreat planning.

www.ingramcontent.com/pod-product-compliance
Lightning Source LLC
Chambersburg PA
CBHW051831160426
43209CB00006B/1124